Shattering Earthquakes

Louise and Richard Spilsbury

www.heinemann.co.uk/library
Visit our website to find out more information about **Heinemann Library** books.

To order:
 Phone 44 (0) 1865 888066
 Send a fax to 44 (0) 1865 314091
💻 Visit the Heinemann Bookshop at www.heinemann.co.uk/library to browse our catalogue and order online.

First published in Great Britain by Heinemann Library, Halley Court, Jordan Hill, Oxford OX2 8EJ, part of Harcourt Education.
Heinemann is a registered trademark of Harcourt Education Ltd.

Editorial: Andrew Farrow and Dan Nunn
Design: David Poole and Paul Myerscough
Illustrations: Geoff Ward
Picture Research: Rebecca Sodergren and Debra Weatherley
Production: Viv Hichens

Originated by Dot Gradations Limited
Printed in Hong Kong, China by Wing King Tong

ISBN 0 431 17836 4
08 07 06 05 04
10 9 8 7 6 5 4 3 2 1

British Library Cataloguing in Publication Data
Spilsbury, Richard, 1963 –
Shattering earthquakes. – (Awesome forces of nature)
1. Earthquakes – Juvenile literature
I. Title II. Spilsbury, Louise
551.2'2
A full catalogue record for this book is available from the British Library.

Acknowledgements
The publishers would like to thank the following for permission to reproduce photographs:

Associated Press pp. **4** (Eric Risberg), **8** (Leonette Medici, Stringer), **14**, **15**, **16** (Paul Sakuma), **19** (John Swart), **22** (Ian McKain); British Geological Survey p. **11**; Corbis pp. **23** (Roger Ressmeyer), **25** (Galen Rowell), **26** (Roger Ressmeyer; FEMA p. **28**; NOAA/ National Geophysical Data Center, Boulder, Colorado pp. **9**, **12**, **15**, **17**; Oxford Scientific Films p. **18**; Rex Features pp. **5** (Sipa Press), **13** (Sipa Press), **20**, **21**, **24** (Sten Rosenlund); Science Photo Library p. **27** (David Parker); Still Pictures pp. **7** (Kevin Schafer).

Cover photograph reproduced courtesy of Associated Press/Wally Santana.

Contents

*Any words appearing in the text in bold, **like this**, are explained in the Glossary.*

What is an earthquake?

Imagine you are reading at a table. You notice that the clock and your glass are beginning to wobble. Then you hear a rumbling sound, like a jet aeroplane flying above the house. Objects in the room rattle and shake more and more. Then, suddenly, your whole room jerks, knocking things off the table and pictures off the walls.

This is how it can feel in an earthquake. An earthquake is when the surface of the Earth moves. The ground under our feet usually feels solid but during an earthquake it shakes, cracks open and dips. Most earthquakes are very small and people may only feel a slight trembling under their feet. Others can make cracks in walls and jolt books off shelves. The worst earthquakes in the world can cause terrible destruction.

In this photo, rescue dogs are being used to search for survivors after an earthquake destroyed houses in San Francisco, USA, in October 1989.

Large earthquakes can transform huge areas of the Earth in an instant. During a major earthquake, the shaking of the Earth can knock down buildings, break open roads and bridges and make huge cracks appear in the land. Cars, buildings and whole lakes can disappear into these cracks.

The huge cracks in this road in Gujarat, India, were caused by a disastrous earthquake in 2001.

What causes earthquakes?

Earthquakes are movements of the ground. They usually happen in certain places because of the way the Earth is made. To understand how earthquakes happen, you need to know a bit about how our planet is formed.

The surface of the Earth is made of a layer of hard rock. This layer forms the land and the floor of the oceans. It is called the **crust**. Under the crust there is more rock. Millions of years ago, this rock cracked, like the shell of an egg. It split into giant pieces called **plates**. These plates float like huge rafts on hot, liquid rock that bubbles deep inside the Earth. They move very, very slowly around the Earth.

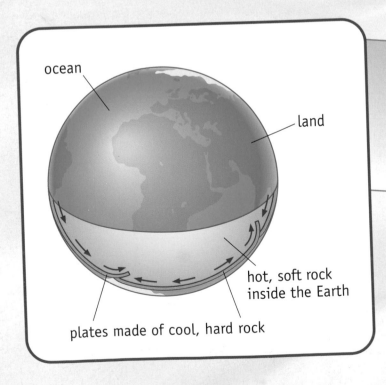

ocean

land

hot, soft rock inside the Earth

plates made of cool, hard rock

The Earth's plates are pieces under the Earth's surface that fit together rather like panels on a football.

Moving plates

As the plates move, they rub or slide against each other. The place where plates meet is called a **fault**. In most places, one plate slides against another in a slow and steady way. Most plates move at a speed of only a few centimetres each year – that's about the same rate of growth as your fingernails!

Sometimes two plates get stuck against each other. For many years they slowly push harder and harder against each other. Then, suddenly, the force becomes too much and these gigantic plates of rock slip past each other. When this happens, the crust above shudders and shakes too. This is an earthquake. The force of the plates suddenly jerking apart can open cracks in the crust above and around the fault.

Fault lines are usually deep underground, but some can be seen on the surface. This is the San Andreas Fault. It runs down the west coast of North America.

Shock waves

The point on the Earth's surface above the start of an earthquake is called the **epicentre**. The force of an earthquake spreads out in waves from the epicentre in all directions. These movements are called **shock waves**. Shock waves ripple through the rocks all round the epicentre like ripples on a pond when you throw in a stone. Shock waves can travel for hundreds of kilometres, but they get weaker as they get further away from the epicentre.

Aftershocks

Earthquakes usually happen in groups. A major earthquake may start off with small earth **tremors** (movements) that gradually get stronger. These may happen several days before the main earthquake happens. After the main quake, there may be **aftershocks**. Many are too small to feel, but others are like smaller earthquakes. They usually occur within a few days, getting weaker over time.

This damage was not caused by a main earthquake. It was caused by aftershocks after an earthquake hit Umbria, Italy in 1997.

Measuring earthquakes

Earthquakes are measured on the **Richter scale**. It is based on the amount of damage they cause. The higher the number on the scale, the more powerful the earthquake is. The weakest earthquake is rated 1 and the strongest earthquake possible would be rated a 10.

What do the ratings mean?

• 2.0 or below – people above ground cannot feel an earthquake like this and it is not recorded.

• Below 4.0 – earthquake can be felt but usually causes little or no damage.

• Over 5.0 – earthquake will be felt by all and could cause some damage.

• Over 6.0 – earthquake that can cause serious damage to buildings.

• Over 7.0 – major earthquake that causes severe damage and can topple buildings.

• Over 8.0 – earthquake that causes almost total destruction in the area it hits.

On 17 August 1999 an earthquake shook the cities of Izmit and Istanbul in Turkey. It measured 7.4 on the Richter scale and caused terrible damage.

Where do earthquakes happen?

Earthquakes can happen all over the Earth, on land or on the ocean floor. Some earthquakes happen in the middle of **plates**. They happen in places where there is a line of weakness in the Earth's **crust**. But most earthquakes happen where two of the Earth's plates meet.

Many earthquakes happen around the edges of the Pacific Ocean. This is where several plates meet and where hot liquid rock can escape to the surface. This means that many earthquakes and **volcanoes** happen in this area, which has been named the 'Ring of Fire'. Another area that suffers from many earthquakes is a zone that runs from Italy and Greece, through central Asia and the Himalayas.

This map shows the area where most of the earthquakes on Earth happen. The red circles mark places where some of the most damaging earthquakes of recent years have happened. Four out of every five earthquakes occur in the Ring of Fire.

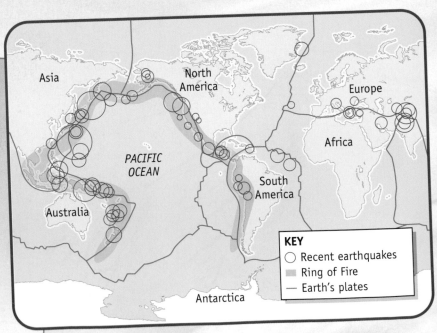

KEY
○ Recent earthquakes
▨ Ring of Fire
— Earth's plates

West Midlands, UK, 2002

Earthquakes can happen in all sorts of places. Few people think of the UK as a country that has earthquakes. In fact, the UK has quite a powerful earthquake every ten years or so. One recent earthquake began at around 1 a.m. on 23 September 2002. Thousands of people woke up to feel their houses and furniture shaking and their windows rattling. The earthquake measured 4.8 on the **Richter scale** and its **epicentre** was in Dudley in the West Midlands. It shook buildings in parts of the West Midlands, Wales, North Yorkshire, London and Wiltshire for up to 30 seconds.

'The house started shaking quite violently. All the power was cut off. Quite a few people came out of their houses wondering what was going on. The streets were in darkness.' Richard Flynn, West Midlands

No-one was hurt in the West Midlands earthquake, but there was some minor damage.

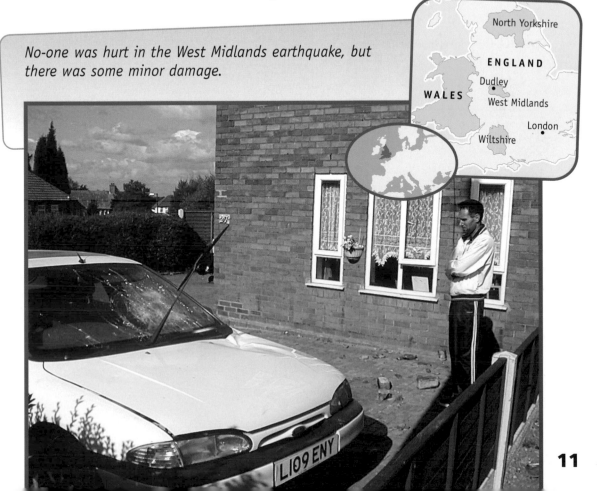

North Yorkshire

ENGLAND

WALES

Dudley

West Midlands

London

Wiltshire

What happens in an earthquake?

Earthquakes usually do most damage at the **epicentre**, but **shock waves** can make land for miles around shake and tremble. In a severe earthquake, the ground can rise and fall like waves in the sea. In the worst cases, the entire shape of the land can be changed.

When an earthquake shakes the ground, it can make walls crack and roofs fall in. If one building falls, it can make the one next to it collapse too. When earthquakes jolt the ground they can break electricity cables and gas pipes. Sparks from electricity cables can cause fires and leaking gas can cause explosions. Earthquakes can rip apart roads and crack and bend bridges. **Aftershocks** bring yet more damage. They make things that were weakened by the first earthquake fall down.

In 1995 an earthquake in Kobe, Japan killed over 5000 people. Many people died because the roofs of buildings fell on them.

Mexico City, 1985

Earthquakes can change landscapes by opening cracks in the Earth and changing land levels. They can also turn firm land into soft, dangerous land.

On 19 September 1985, a huge earthquake hit Mexico City. The **epicentre** was 50 kilometres off the coast in the sea. However, the quake still rated 8.1 on the **Richter scale** when it reached Mexico City, over 300 kilometres inland. The earthquake was so bad because the city sits on soil made of soft sand and clay. The **shock waves** shook the soil grains apart, turning it into quicksand. This caused buildings to tilt, shift or even sink into it. Over 10,000 people were killed, over 40,000 people were injured, and around 100,000 people were left homeless.

Once the dust clouds had cleared, it became obvious that much of Mexico City had been reduced to rubble.

Do earthquakes cause other disasters?

Earthquakes do not just break or bury buildings, bridges and roads. They can also set off other disasters such as **landslides**. When a hill is damaged and shaken up by an earthquake, the soil on the side of the hill can slide down. This can cause a huge landslide or mudslide. When large amounts of sand or soil fall like this they can bury people or buildings at the bottom of the hillside.

The town beneath the sea!

In 1692 an earthquake started a landslide in a town called Port Royal on the island of Jamaica. The whole town slid into the sea and became buried in the seabed. It was not until 1959 that divers found objects from this lost city, on the sea floor.

In 2001 an earthquake rocked El Salvador. It caused a landslide that buried the small town of Las Colinas. The landslide buried hundreds of houses and killed 315 people.

Earthquakes under the sea

Earthquakes do not only happen on land. They also happen under the sea. When an earthquake happens deep under the water, it creates giant waves called **tsunamis**. Most tsunamis are barely noticeable in deep parts of oceans, but they get bigger as they approach land. When tsunamis hit a coastline they can become like huge walls of water. They sweep away, crush or flood anything in their path.

The largest earthquake ever recorded measured 9.5 on the **Richter scale**! It struck on 22 May 1960 off the coast of southern Chile, causing terrible damage in Chile. It also created a tsunami that caused great destruction all around the Pacific Ocean, especially in Hawaii and Japan.

In July 1998, a tsunami struck Sissano in northern Papua New Guinea. Many houses were swept away by the water, and thousands of people were injured or killed.

San Francisco, USA, 1989

The American city of San Francisco lies on the San Andreas **Fault** and has had several gigantic earthquakes in the past. On 17 October 1989 another huge earthquake hit the city. The **epicentre** was near Santa Cruz, but the earthquake also affected San Francisco and Oakland, 80 kilometres away.

It was early evening – around 5 p.m. – and San Francisco was busy. Many fans were packed into the city's baseball stadium ready to watch a World Series match and many city workers were on their way home. The earthquake lasted less than 20 seconds and rated 7.1 on the **Richter scale**. Around 60 people were killed, over 3000 people were injured and around US$10 billion worth of damage was caused.

The top deck of this road collapsed onto the lower deck when the earth shook. Cars were crushed, 42 people were killed and 200 people were injured. This road was later demolished.

USA

San Francisco
Oakland
× epicentre
Santa Cruz

CALIFORNIA

PACIFIC OCEAN

Different kinds of damage

There were scenes of destruction all down the Californian coast. In the Santa Cruz mountains, a building slid all the way down a hillside. The earthquake also created cracks in the mountainside. One person who lived on the mountains said, 'I can't stop shaking. I guess I'm surviving, but I'm scared.'

Many roads were cracked or split; **landslides** or rockslides blocked others. Over 90 bridges in the area were damaged and San Francisco's Bay Bridge was closed for months. Many mobile homes, buildings and businesses were destroyed. Other buildings buckled and bent. The earthquake cracked gas pipes, which led to fires in one area. Water pipes were also damaged so firefighters had to pump seawater from San Francisco Bay to put out the fires.

This building was actually shifted onto a car by the immense land movements caused by the Santa Cruz earthquake.

Who helps after an earthquake?

Most earthquakes are over in a matter of seconds, but they can cause terrible damage and destruction. The first job after a major earthquake is to rescue survivors and prevent other disasters, such as fires, from causing further damage.

Rescue workers

Firefighters, the army and **volunteers** all work to rescue people trapped in their homes or cars. They may use specially trained dogs to find people by sniffing them out. Often, rescue workers have to use heavy lifting and cutting equipment to get people out from under crushed buildings or fallen bridges. Damage to buildings and roads after an earthquake may make emergency work more difficult. For example, blocked roads stop firefighters reaching fires. Construction workers may have to bring cranes and diggers to clear roads first. Rescue work is very dangerous because **aftershocks** can be devastating too.

This French rescue team is searching for survivors after an earthquake in India. Their dogs can smell people trapped under the rubble.

Helping people

Ambulances try to arrive at the scene as quickly as possible. Ambulance staff give emergency medical treatment and take injured people away to hospital. Workers from the Red Cross and other **aid organizations** also help after earthquakes. As well as giving **first aid**, they provide people whose homes have been destroyed with somewhere to stay and food to eat.

The work does not stop after everyone has been rescued or taken to hospital. New homes have to be built for people who have lost their homes. Aid organizations help people who have become separated from their families to find them again. People may have also lost their businesses or shops. Often ordinary people send money to help earthquake victims rebuild their lives.

After an earthquake, workers have to clear up the rubble from wrecked buildings and roads. They also check that any buildings left standing are safe enough for people to move back in to.

Iran, 1990

At 12.30 a.m. on 21 June 1990 an earthquake blasted through north-west Iran. It rated 7.7 on the **Richter scale** and was the worst earthquake in the country for twelve years. The earthquake killed 50,000 people, injured 200,000 more and made half a million homeless.

The first earthquake lasted a whole minute. Then there were twelve **aftershocks** – one was three days after the first aftershock. Whole towns and villages were destroyed. In one area a **dam** was shaken so badly that water spilled out. This caused floods that killed many people.

In towns like this one every single building was flattened and almost everyone living there was killed.

Rescue operations

There was so much rubble blocking roads that workers had to use bulldozers to clear it away so that ambulances and other rescue vehicles could get to areas where people needed help. In areas where emergency services could not get through to help, **volunteers** used their bare hands to rescue families that were trapped.

Other workers used cranes to lift slabs of concrete to set people free. The rescue workers faced many difficulties. For example, the earthquake broke lots of underground pipes so many areas did not have any water or electricity for days or even weeks.

*After the Iran earthquake, the Red Cross **aid organization** flew in trained medical workers and supplies by helicopter.*

Can earthquakes be predicted?

It is very hard to tell when and where an earthquake will happen. Sometimes there are small **tremors**. Often, animals behave oddly before an earthquake – dogs bark wildly, horses rear up and snakes, mice and rats come out of their holes. However, these things do not always happen. Even if they do, it may be too close to the actual earthquake for there to be enough time to escape.

Studying earthquakes

Scientists who study earthquakes are called **seismologists**. They use machines called **seismometers** to measure shaking of the ground. They gather information from thousands of seismometers all around the world. Using maps that show where the world's **faults** are, seismologists study slight movements of the ground. If there is more shaking and ground movement than usual, an earthquake is more likely.

This is a chart made by a seismometer. The squiggly lines show that the ground has moved. The more the ground shakes, the larger the squiggle.

Seismometers provide useful information about an earthquake as it happens. But scientists are also working on ways of predicting earthquakes. One way is using information collected by **satellites** above the Earth. Special cameras in the satellites measure the shape of the Earth's crust. These measurements show if there are small changes that could warn of an earthquake. Scientists hope that this information will be able to help them to predict some earthquakes in the future.

A success story

A warning to **evacuate** was given to the people of Haicheng in China several days before a bad earthquake in 1975. There had been several warning signs, including animals behaving oddly, land shifting, water seeping out of the ground and small tremors. When these tremors got stronger, the warning was given and many lives were saved. Unfortunately, most earthquakes do not give such clear warning signals.

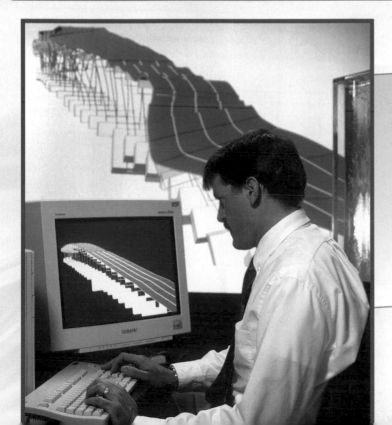

This scientist is using a computer to study the effects of an earthquake on a bridge in San Francisco, USA. This will enable engineers to make the bridge safer in the future.

Can people prepare for earthquakes?

At present it is almost impossible to predict that an earthquake is definitely going to happen. The best way to reduce the amount of damage earthquakes cause is for everyone to be well prepared.

Making buildings safer

One of the greatest causes of death in an earthquake is people being crushed under buildings. One of the main ways of saving lives is to build homes and other buildings that are strong enough to cope with earthquakes. Even in the strongest quakes, these should at least stay standing long enough for people to escape. Designers create buildings that can move slightly in an earthquake without breaking up.

In the Loma Prieta earthquake in 1989, the Transamerica Pyramid in San Francisco shook badly. However, the building was not damaged and no one was hurt. This 49-storey office building has special supports at its base that protect it from the ground-shuddering effects of earthquakes.

The most important thing builders have to consider is the land they are about to build on. Tall buildings should never be placed on loose soil that might sink and shift in an earthquake. When people make bridges or office blocks with metal frames they should include rubber pads to absorb the **shocks** of an earthquake. This allows the building to move slightly with the shaking, rather than breaking up.

What about poorer countries?

Unfortunately, many earthquakes happen in places where people cannot afford to pay for safety measures like these. Poorer people may have no choice about the materials with which they build their homes. In Peru, millions of people live in cheap **adobe** (mud) houses. These often fall down in earthquakes because the walls are not connected together and mud is a weak building material.

One way of strengthening mud buildings like these in Peru is to join edges with a mesh of wire and cover them with concrete. However, even this cheap solution costs too much for many people.

How should people prepare?

People who live in earthquake zones should not worry about earthquakes. But everyone in the family should learn exactly what to do. They should all know how to **evacuate**. They should know a safe place to go to and a safe route to get there. Local government offices can give people information about what to do in an earthquake.

Things to do to prepare

There are several ways people can make the insides of their homes safer. Things that can fall, break or start fires may injure people. So, people should bolt or strap heaters, cupboards and bookcases to walls to stop them falling. It is also a good idea to keep heavy objects on the bottom shelves, and to hang pictures and mirrors away from beds.

This team is reinforcing the basement of a house so it can withstand earthquakes better.

What to do in an earthquake

One way of being prepared is knowing what to do in an earthquake. Here are some tips to remember:

- Try not to panic. Earthquakes are scary, but they usually only last a few seconds.

- If you are indoors take cover immediately under a strong table or desk. Stay away from glass, windows or anything that could fall, like a bookcase.

- If you are outdoors, move away from buildings, street lights, telephone wires and **power lines**.

- If you are in a crowded place, don't rush for the doors if everyone else is doing that. Never get into a lift.

- Don't forget that there may be **aftershocks** following an earthquake. Aftershocks can cause things that were weakened by the main earthquake to fall down.

These schoolchildren are being taught what to do in the event of an earthquake. One of the most important things to remember is to duck and cover. Get down and get cover to protect yourself from falling objects.

Can earthquakes be prevented?

An earthquake is an awesome force of nature that people cannot control. Earthquakes have always happened and always will. To limit the damage earthquakes cause, people must understand the dangers. They should also build or alter their homes to make them less likely to fall down when an earthquake happens.

At present, **scientists** can only say roughly where an earthquake might occur. They cannot be sure about when it might happen. In the future, scientists hope to set up systems across the world that can more accurately predict earthquakes. If this happens they will be able to warn people to **evacuate** before an earthquake begins.

In order to reduce the amount of damage earthquakes can do, people need to learn what earthquakes are and what to do if an earthquake happens in their area.

Major earthquakes of the recent past

Chile, 1960
In May 1960 the world's strongest recorded earthquake – 9.5 on the **Richter scale** – hit Chile. A 10-metre high **tsunami** wiped out whole villages in Chile and killed 122 more people when it hit Japan.

Tangshan, China, 1976
The Chinese city of Tangshan was reduced to rubble in an earthquake that killed between 200,000 and 500,000 people.

Armenia, 1988
In December 1988, an earthquake measuring 6.9 on the Richter scale hit north-west Armenia, killing 25,000 people.

Makarashtra, India, 1993
Around 10,000 villagers were killed and 65 villages destroyed during an earthquake in south-west India in September 1993.

Kobe, Japan, 1995
In January 1995, 5500 people were killed after the Hyogo earthquake in Kobe.

Iran, 1997
In February 1997 an earthquake measuring 5.5 on the Richter scale killed 1000 people. Three months later a stronger tremor, measuring 7.1, killed 1560 more.

Northern Afghanistan, 1998
An earthquake in Northern Afghanistan killed 4000 people on 30 May 1998.

Turkey, 1999
On 17 August 1999 an earthquake measuring 7.4 on the Richter scale shook the cities of Izmit and Istanbul, killing over 17,000 people and injuring tens of thousands more.

Gujarat, India, 2001
An earthquake in Gujarat, India killed over 20,000 people and injured more than 100,000 people.

Glossary

adobe clay used to make bricks that are dried in the sun

aftershock small tremors or ground movements that happen soon after the main jolt of an earthquake

aid organizations groups of people who work together to raise money and to provide help for people in need

crust layer of rock that forms the land we live on and the floor of the oceans

dam barrier built to hold back water to create a reservoir or to prevent flooding in an area

epicentre point on the Earth's surface above the start of an earthquake

evacuate/evacuation when people move from a dangerous place to somewhere they will be safe

fault place where two or more different plates meet below the Earth's crust

first aid first medical help given to injured people

landslides when heavy rains and wind make large amounts of mud and rock slide down a hill or mountain

plates the rocky layer that forms the surface of the Earth is split into giant pieces. These pieces are called plates.

power lines main cables that carry electricity

Richter scale scale that tells people how powerful an earthquake is

satellite object that goes around the Earth in space. Satellites do jobs such as sending out TV signals or taking photographs.

scientist person who studies aspects of the world around us

seismologist scientist who studies earthquakes

seismometer machine that measures the shaking of the ground

shock violent shaking movement caused by an earthquake

shock waves movements through the ground caused by an earthquake. Shock waves ripple through rocks all round the epicentre like ripples on a pond.

tremor shaking of the ground

tsunami giant wave caused by an earthquake or other disturbance, such as a landslide

volcano when hot liquid rock from the centre of the Earth spurts out from a hole in the Earth's crust

volunteers people who work without being paid for what they do

Find out more

Books

Eyewitness Guides: Volcano and Earthquake, Susanna Van Rose (Dorling Kindersley, 2000)

Earth-shattering Earthquakes (Horrible Geography), Anita Ganeri (Scholastic Hippo, 2000)

Earthquakes and Volcanoes (Understanding Geography), F. Watt (Usborne Publishing, 1994)

Websites

www.howstuffworks.com/earthquake.htm – visit this website to find out more about how earthquakes work.

www.fema.gov/hazards/earthquakes – the FEMA website contains useful facts about earthquake dangers, what to do and how to prepare.

www.earthquake.usgs.gov/4kids/ – a website about earthquakes produced by the US Geological Survey.

www.nationalgeographic.com/education/homework/index.html – to see a video of an earthquake happening go to the 'Science/Nature' section and look under earthquakes.

Index

Titles in the *Awesome Forces of Nature* series include:

Hardback   0 431 17828 3

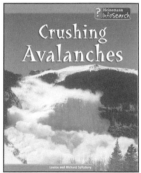

Hardback   0 431 17831 3

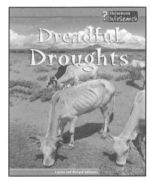

Hardback   0 431 17829 1

Hardback   0 431 17835 6

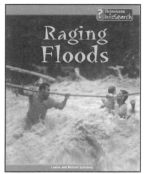

Hardback   0 431 17830 5

Hardback   0 431 17836 4

Hardback   0 431 17832 1

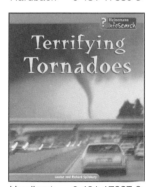

Hardback   0 431 17837 2

Hardback   0 431 17838 0

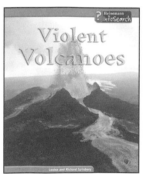

Hardback   0 431 17834 8

Find out about the other titles in this series on our website
www.heinemann.co.uk/library